The Art of Drinking Wine

(LIKE THE FRENCH DO)

MONSEIGNEUR LE VIN

The Art of Drinking Wine

(LIKE THE FRENCH DO)

PREPARE
SERVE
DRINK

Text by
LOUIS FOREST

Illustrations by
CHARLES MARTIN

New York Paris London Milan

TABLE OF CONTENTS

* Translations for original illustrated text appear with an asterisk

PREFACE

Opening

A proverb says: "When wine is opened, you must drink it."
This maxim is deplorable.

Obviously, it cannot have been the product of a discerning mind with a discerning palate. A gourmand would have written: "When wine is opened, you must know how to drink it!"

The Civilized Drinker

Here is an exceptionally important distinction: There is a marked difference between the banal drinker who gulps, guzzles, and swigs and the tasteful man who tenderly savors a masterpiece of the vineyard while also sharing with amateurs worthy of his trust the assessments and the comparisons that inform an important determination, all the while allowing the taste buds to be stimulated!

Le buveur civilisé

* *The Civilized Drinker*

No excess

This little book isn't geared toward problem drinkers or casual consumers. It exists for the dandies of drinking, for the exceptional gourmand; it is the conscious gourmand whom I'd

le Champion
du Sec
Regime

le
Gouliafre

like to address. For the record—and this is important—I'm a sober gourmet. I hate all excess (which is a kind of tactlessness) and I profess my belief in the true religion of equilibrium to which I've devoted my faith. Epicurus said: "Practice moderation in tasting the fullness of life's pleasures!'" So: I'm neither a barfly nor a voracious eater who would proclaim the profound beauty of classic wine here. When—slowly, blissfully, passionately, seriously, lovingly—I respectfully, mystically, delectably bring to my mouth a glass of wine in which the chosen land, the fortifying sun, the traditional experience, the care of experts, and the maturing years enjoyed their best collaboration, when the nose, or better yet, the *discerning* nose inhales and classifies the quasi-musical sensations; indeed, I can attest that the resulting happiness isn't only physical; it deeply stirs the soul!

Education

Unfortunately, many people close themselves off to the unknown that can, upon first impression, seem arcane or impenetrable. It's often simply a matter of education! The instructor made a mistake. Nobody revealed the hidden beauties. Henceforth, we'll review them as those people walk, emotionless, across ground under which sleeps a buried treasure that is unable to tempt, because it is ignored!

Often, the gift of understanding the civilization of the mouth, the nose, the tongue, and taste is missing—grasping these nuances is a sort of poetry. In this case, there's nothing to do but dismiss the pupil, who, depending on temperament, will become a drunkard or—which comes down to the same thing in the grand scheme of things—a champion of sobriety, back to their humble origins.

In France, the vine has a time-honored richness. During their greatest era of power, the Romans imported wines of great renown from the Gauls. In the Middle Ages, the celebrated crus were saintly property. Monks carefully passed down the laws of scrupulous winemaking, because there isn't a more difficult art form than that of making, conserving, and serving of wine. It requires determination, instinct, science, time, patience, and love!

Today we still glory in the fruits of passionate winegrowers, worthy of our ancestors, but with many producers sloppily remaining loyal to vine stocks and wine presses, their clientele lost the necessary connoisseurship needed to understand wine. In years gone by, enthusiasts were educated early on.

———

Roast Pig

One copy of a small book from the end of the seventeenth century exists, but only one copy; an extraordinary rarity conserved in a state library, entitled *Roast Pig*.

It's the first known alphabet primer. It was used to teach reading to the children of Bourgogne, a region where wine gourmets are said to have "silk intestines," so impressive is their appreciation of quality. All of the scholarly examples in the book were intended to teach the best precepts of good living, good cooking, and how to drink properly. On one page—I'm keeping the naively incorrect text—it reads:

The grape was always consecrated to God. White and red grapes are used to make good wine, which is necessary for Altars; it makes man's heart rejoice, provides milk to old men, is nectar at meals, and forms strong blood when it's consumed in this respect. But it spoils everyone when you drink too much of it.

You see? In the good old days we knew how to educate our youth.

And isn't it incredible that, in a country like ours, ignorance about wine is so common, and it's so badly taught, and, despite one thousand foreign advertisements meant to kill our spirits, our crus are the best in the world, and our "small" wines are still "big" wines compared to all the others. They're little only because they're next to the great ones!

This pedagogical shortcoming is strange in a country where the vine reigns in all four geographical corners, surrounding a surprising center of miraculous climbing vines. We teach children that King Clovis, a proud Sicambrian, was once going to convert and anoint himself in Reims, yet we forget to mention that the bishop of Reims was one of the greatest wine growers of his time, a virtue that was tied to Clovis's enthusiasm.

Because we're pushing absurdity to a point where we no longer teach of our vines' glory, the several pages that you'll read aim to supplant this ignorance; but today I'll settle for a sole chapter covering a vast treatise that will discuss "The Art of Drinking Wine."

PART ONE

Prepare

CHAPTER I

The wine cellar

Here, I won't discuss the care vines demand, nor the challenges of the grape harvest, nor the precautions demanded by an ideal wine-making process, nor the one hundred thousand concepts that a winemaker who wants the wine served at your table to not be a random glass filled with vinegar, cheap wine made of log wood, tasting of hard

21

acid or grease, but an object of gustatory taste, a supreme delectation, you know, a real "bottle."

I also won't tell you what your wine cellar should be.

Alas! Parisians are going to read these lines! Barring exceptions to prove the rule, does one still know what a wine cellar is in Paris? . . . A wine cellar: its thick walls, shadows, peaceful vibrations, perfectly balanced temperature.

Paris vibrates; its ground shivers; buses disturb liquids' sleep. Cellar furnaces overheat; underground passages are sewers through which electronic pipes run, whose questionable influence has far-reaching effects on wine, which is sensitive like a coquette.

What happened to the times when the wine cellar, which the Belgians still call the "library," was a venerated place, even in Paris?

Within it, bottles were lined up and respected, like a brood of children. Their noble, dusty immobility told marvelous stories to connoisseurs.

Therefore, even if you don't have a wine cellar, but you're one of those individuals possessing the vague notion that wine is better than booze, as organ music is superior to noise, and you're aware of your ignorance, I dare hope to transform you into a disciple of the beverage that is the most spiritual of the spirits, and herewith I'll open the gates of the temple for you!

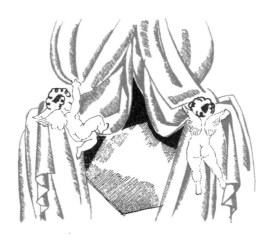

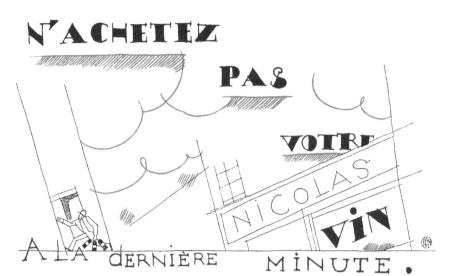

CHAPTER II

Buying Wine

First off, avoid the elementary mistake of buying wine at the last minute. Wine certainly isn't afraid of traveling. In times past, refined people would have their wine take a long back-and-forth trip to the Indies to improve it; but when it's displaced it requires a rest, oftentimes long before the hour when it's sacrificed for pleasure. The only time great wines

Le vin doit être vieux

taste nasty is when harried amateurs uncork them too soon after receiving them!

I know of certain beautiful bottles of Bourgogne whose idleness, following a long trip, took more than a year to satisfy the re-establishment of their integral beauty.

If you have friends over to dine, you shouldn't go fetch the wine when you sit down at the table, because even if you have the right to drink badly, you never have the right to let others drink badly.

Let the old bottles relax as much as possible, for at least eight days.

They will reward you for this solitude by awakening in beauty.

Now for a digression. Don't be suspect of wine that's too old. Old? Yes,

mais point sénile

* Wine must be old (top), but not senile (bottom)

old—but not senile. The label's antiquity results only in bitter regret when the liquid of the glorious name breathlessly passes away in your glass, finished! Wine should be an old man who, maintaining his lucidity, tells of his long existence, his maturity, with a smile; but don't wait to introduce this charming chatterbox, before he's dead. A dinner is a generous conversation rather than a funeral. You see, it's best to serve wine that's too young rather than too old.

It's certain that it's only when the aging, through the addition of infinite oxidations, has fruitified the molecules as perfectly as possible, that a great wine is worthy of a great table!

From the bottle to the wine glass, From the wine glass to the lips

The host, steeped in the honor owed to their guests, who do them the honor of sitting at their table, doesn't just settle for purchasing well-bred bottles. Even if the bottles contained the finest, most quintessential flower nectar from the most beautiful centuries, the host's duty would only be beginning. To be sent a wine worthy of this title by an expert, honest, and choice supplier is excellent. But it isn't everything.

It's said that the space between the wine glass and the lips is large; but the route is even more delicate between the bottle and the wine glass. I will try to serve as a guide for these two difficult voyages.

————

L'ÉLUE

CHAPTER III

The Preparation Itself

Let's say that you have a mature red wine to serve: a Bourgogne, well-rounded, sensual, voluptuous like a man, or a Bordeaux, flexible, harmonious, voluptuous like a woman. I'm mentioning these two types of wine because one can't cover everything; but this truth applies to other crus, whether it's Côtes du Rhône, full of vigor like their sunlight, or other climbing vines that are strong enough to slowly age without spoiling.

The "bottle" was selected in accordance to the menu, and the guests. We already know which bottle will be the victim of a beautiful sacrifice.

But you still need to transport the mature red wine from the wine cellar or pantry to the site of consumption. Be careful! It's delicate.

The Decanting

Older red wines require decanting. Over time they leave sediment at the bottom of the bottles. The cloudless liquid needs to be separated from this bastard residue. With this goal in mind, the wine is carefully decanted while taking every precaution so that the invading material doesn't get swept into the stream of liquid. Most often, the wine is transferred from the bottle to a carafe.

But from here I can perceive the irate gaze of the elderly winemaker who cries out: "Monsieur, you must never decant! Whoever decants becomes disillusioned! Excuse me! You're going to serve wine from a carafe? How?! You're not going to let your guests see the bottle, which becomes dressed in noble dust over time? Pardon! You wish to deprive us of this experience that awakens the Bacchanalian appetite? But the bottle already inspires dreams! It evokes the grape harvest, the ancestral vines, the noble cru, the rare year, success, the long, long, long sleep of the liquid that will wake up one last time, for a short but splendid sensation! By decanting into a carafe, you lose the essential emotion. No, no, the winemaker himself goes to the cellar. With fervent attention, he extracts the bottle from the precious racks; with a quick gesture, he takes care to mix the dense liquids separated through aging. Without turning the bottle, without stirring or bringing it to its side, he horizontally stores it in a wicker basket, on the same side where it will remain. He carries it to the place where it will be consumed, one, two, or three hours before the appointed time. When the time comes, he proudly presents it to his guests, who are enraptured. Next, he completes the crucial uncorking process with a calculated

RÈGLE DE NOBLESSE

slowness. He nervously inhales, the cork hardens—and after, reassured and certain that the beautiful liquid won't smell like the cork, he slowly pours the wine into glasses. With the look of a goldsmith weighing precious stones, he breathlessly watches the purple-hued flow. As soon as a suspected piece of sediment appears, he straightens the bottle's neck and turns it upright, which has now finished its job, after which, he breathes more easily, and victoriously glances at the radiant drinkers. Such is the noble rule."

* Noble Rule

This is how the old, expert winemaker speaks; he simply forgets that in reality, he himself has just decanted wine. His painstaking precautions are a form of decantation.

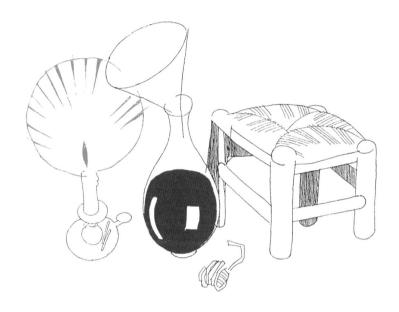

Unfortunately, it's not always easy to observe all the necessary religious rites. This fervor is only possible when the faithful are in small number. Most often, this way of drinking isn't practical. It barely suits cities or large receptions, where the dining arrangement doesn't allow for a sommelier for each bottle. In this case, and often in others, decanting into a carafe is necessary. A friend of mine, an ophthalmologist with a fine nose, one day described to me the first part of decanting in the following way: "The operator stands in front of the wine rack; he's carrying a "cellar rat" candlestick and nearby is a stool of eight to ten inches.

Operation

A. – Take the bottle out of the rack while keeping it strictly horizontal; if it's coming from the row in front, as soon as the cork has cleared the rack, always horizontally lower the bottle, or lift it, after taking it by the bottom or top, until it's at the same level of the middle left thigh of the "officiant." This individual will lift their leg, placing the foot on the stool, so that the thigh angles at forty-five degrees.

B. – Incline the bottle's bottom backwards until it can rest on the lifted thigh. With the help of a levered corkscrew, unscrew the cork without shaking. Once this is done, bring the bottle's neck close to the carafe, and decant the wine while avoiding any collisions and verifying the level of sediment with the candlestick placed underneath the bottle.

C. – It goes without saying that when a bottle is in a back row, the manipulation, which is exactly the same, needs to be preceded by a horizontal rotation of the bottle, so that it can be fully flipped. With this process, easier to do than to describe, you can decant with a minimum of movement, and, consequently, a minimal chance of troubling the wine."

Déboucher

* Uncork

Another Way of Decanting

For decanting in a wine cellar, the first rule is: have a wine cellar! But, as I've said, the wine cellar is dying, the wine cellar is dead! This mathematical and social law can be proven: building a wine cellar is in direct opposition to building a bathroom.

As we must not allow hydrotherapy—water, wine's enemy—to deprive us of great bottles, here is a feasible method of decanting for apartment-dwelling gourmets.

A. — Keep the bottle upright for three or four days before you plan to uncork it; keep it immobile. In this position, the sediment will slowly fall to the bottom.

B. — Uncork with meticulous attention, taking the utmost care to not shake the delicate vessel, and smell the cork.

C. — When decanting, light a candle and examine the bottom of the bottle with the flame, to determine on which side the sediment is the thickest.

D. — Unless it's indicated later on, prepare the carafe that will be served at the table, and top it off with a funnel. Place the lit candle to the right of the carafe. With your right hand hold the bottle at its butt (excuse this inconvenient word, short, sonorous, but technical) while making sure

Sentir le bouchon

* Smell the cork

the side where the sediment is the thickest (see step *C*) stays at the bottom.

Gently tilt the bottle using the left hand's index finger as a pressure point on the neck; tip the bottle a little more while bringing the opening's lips onto the glass's funnel. Open your eyes! The decanting is beginning.

E. — Slowly, slowly, slowly, slowly pour; the air should enter the bottle via tiny bubbles; any "gurgling" unveils angry haste. When the wine napkin reaches its greatest horizontal length, you can speed up a little bit; at this moment, the candle's glow underneath should illuminate the bottle mid-height if it's a Bourgogne, and two-thirds of the way up if you're decanting a Bordeaux; watch out for the progression of small sediment flakes that treacherously make their way to the opening; reduce the pouring speed so that the small flakes remain in the bottle and aren't carried out with the last drops; if, despite everything, this residue appears at the opening, lift the bottle up quickly. Not even an atom of sediment should smudge the visual purity of the wine in the carafe.

This process is complicated to explain, but simple to do. When it's done correctly, the waste remains insignificant. It should fill in a shot glass.

F. — Plug the carafe with some cotton wadding. This plug prevents dust from getting into the liquid. You shouldn't

Verser lentement

* Pour slowly

push it in too tightly; air needs to circulate and oxidize the decanted wine, as it's said elsewhere, to the greatest glory of God . . . let's add: and of humanity!

The Bouquet

Preparing the decanting carafe

In every great bottle, there's a marvelous mystery that the poets of the mouth have called: *the bouquet*. This small genie, which is the wine's scent, is extraordinarily sensitive.

It fears humidity, cold, and heat—for no discernible reason, it can wither, and hide—and this delicate thing needs to be treated with infinite care.

At a restaurant, when you order a valuable cru, the sommelier often brings you a small bottle that's been delicately placed in a bucket. But when it's cold, does the bucket make it better? . . . Sometimes someone will say that the bottle was "brought to room temperature." But what does that mean? More often than not, the bottle was placed close to a fire. The wine arrives lukewarm; it's atrocious! Heating isn't the same as bringing something to room temperature.

If you'd like for the little genie to appear in all of his abundance, you must coax him in the exact way that I'll describe. Right before a meal, you'll fill a carafe with the hottest water that the crystal can take; after several minutes, pour out the water. Take the wine bottle and pour half a glass into the scalding carafe, taking care to shake it in all directions. Thanks to this action, all of the carafe's sides will be immersed in scent. Then, slowly decant the rest of the bottle.

If you practice according to this method, the wine bouquet, the little genie, comes out of his deep hiding place, strolls about, and declares himself satisfied upon arriving in this temperate, aromatic atmosphere; the only thing left to do is to sing his praises!

This problem of the bouquet is so significant that I'll permit myself to add the opinion of the greatly experienced Bourguignon connoisseur, M. Charles Brunot. He writes: "This 'bouquet' is composed of instable ethers. Divine, the product of celestial alcohols, they need oxygen to grow, and a light accentuation of heat to evaporate. Decanting's goal isn't just to leave sediment at the bottom of the bottle. It also allows the ether molecules to oxidize while making contact with oxygen and air. Unless you allow each gulp to stay in your mouth for a long time, or you warm the wine with your hands before swallowing, the evaporation takes place too late. It gets lost, without any benefit, in the stomach.

Therefore, it's necessary to take the precaution of initiating this evaporation with a temperature elevation, early on and discreetly."

These are the general rules.

Now, here are several particular directives.

Youthful and full-bodied, red wines should be uncorked long before lighter or subtler bottles. Sometimes, you can let them take in some fresh air for an entire day before their hour of pleasure.

The serious reds do best when they're uncorked twelve or sometimes even twenty-four hours beforehand. However, the Margaux, Ludon, etc. wines become depleted from lengthy oxidations (except, however, for the very strong years). The Paulliac, Saint-Julien, and Saint-Estèphe wines generally make do with airing out for six to eight hours. As for the Saint-Émilions and Pomerols, they need longer.

Of course, these directives aren't at all definitive; it's for the enlightened connoisseur to determine the necessary oxidation time for each bottle's little genie to achieve the apogee of his greatness.

For red Bourgognes, you generally don't uncork them until the last minute; aeration, or oxidation, is to be avoided. There are exceptions, however.

Sometimes, due to the thermometer's, or, nay, the barometer's, whim, wine can actually be too fresh. The solution to this is simple. As already explained, the drinker warms the glass between the hands. Certain specialists love to coddle their pleasure this way. These are generally lovers of the vine, those who drink while "closing" their eyes to "listen to" the wine!

White wines shouldn't be decanted.

The Temperature

A *red Bordeaux* needs to be brought to room temperature, meaning gently bringing them to a temperature as warm as the place where it'll be consumed.

A *red Bourgogne* is imbibed at a temperature slightly lower than that of the room.

As for *white Bordeaux,* the more lofty its origins, the more it should be consumed cold. Cooling doesn't suffice. You need to chill it. To do so, uncork the bottle before placing it in an ice bucket; then simply replace the cork. Avoid oxidation; meaning, and I'll repeat it, airing it.

45

A *white Bourgogne* is served fresh, but not chilled. Uncork at the last minute. Avoid oxidization.

Champagne is served chilled, but this isn't a new trend. We have documentation dating back to June 1667. It reads:

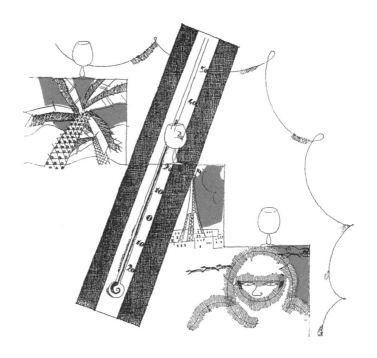

"We have saved the winter ice to temper summer's heat. Our wines will be fresh and delicious."

To chill a wine, take it out twenty minutes before tasting. Place it in a respectfully prepared ice bucket. Uncork; gently put the cork back in. The wine should be neither too cold nor not cold enough!

Other white wines do best when they're fresh: wine from Anjou, Touraine, Alsace, the Rhine, etc.

White Porto is served slightly cooler than the temperature of the room; a little less for red. If there's sediment, you can decant. Porto is indifferent to oxidation, but it's very sensitive to cold.

Madeira is served five or six degrees warmer than the place where it's consumed.

If it's sweet, *Jerez* is best five degrees higher than the place where it's consumed; if it's dry, five degrees lower.

Fortified wines: Muscat, Banyuls, Malaga, etc., should be enjoyed at room temperature.

———

PART TWO

Serve

CHAPTER IV

———

Serving Wine

Glasses and Crystalware

You can recognize a wine dandy by the glass from which he drinks. The habit doesn't make the monk, but the monk doesn't exist without his habit! Yet, how many heresies have modern crystalware committed because of ignorance about wine? You'd think that glassmakers never drink!

First off, let's be clear that stemless glasses don't work for choice wines. Their ungainly form works for those with rude hands, who shatter their glasses on tables after ingurgitating drink. Their only redeemable use is by transatlantic ocean liner restaurants, for which they're a necessity, but how can

évitez

Le Verre sans pied

these glasses pretend to hold the honor of transmitting a noble product to worthy lips? However much they're refined, their elementary harshness lessened, stemless glasses work only for men without detachable collars. Take it from me: stemless glasses are never the correct choice.

They're afflicted by another flaw that's even more serious. A glass should let you admire the wine. That's its first job. With stemless glasses, fingers hide the light.

This obvious fault reveals the justified disdain one should have for this type of glass.

Ah! Certainly, during the Great War, we were less finicky. We drank out of bottles, rationed in quarter liters, in whatever we could find. The spirit of vino was released, despite all the rusted iron and chipped bowls. We were at war!

* Avoid the glass without feet

Today, we endeavor to enliven civilization again. This delicate flower calls for a sense of nuance, choice, perfection.

The stricture forbidding stemless glasses also pertains to colored glasses. Why, you might ask? With infinite finesse, nature distills inspirational colors, so why would you go and destroy this wonderment? Wine's beautiful color brims with anticipated contemplation, and you would go and ruin the enjoyment of this great harmony with opaque and colored things? Break glasses that aren't transparent! As with love, tasting begins with the eyes!

The rule is: no optical interference. The glass or crystal's material should appear to be absent; it should be the most transparent possible and the highest quality available. Whoever loves wine will examine it. Tasting can't exist without the caress of the eyes.

Would you like a demonstration? Since time immemorial, official tasters have availed themselves of silver wine tasters, many of which are works of art. Yes, they are opaque, but the bottom admirably mirrors and reflects the wine's moving nuances with its curving, gleaming metal.

A beautiful glass results from this type of perfection. As radiant as possible, as pure as imaginable, as fine as a strand of hair, it should pardon its presence by allowing us to forget it.

Le Verre Gravé

Let's add that even the smallest embellishment produces a negative impact. An engraved detail can disrupt harmonious simplicity. All the more reason to avoid ribbing, embossing, and bulges of crystal that break a glass's beautiful, geometric curves. Wine doesn't need any other orna-ment than wine itself. It carries all gracefulness within itself.

The kind of glass that's not an eyesore should neither interrupt the second round of pleasure, that of smell. Refined aficianados know that much of the pleasure of wine often lies less in it's imbibing than in its glorious aromas. For the sophisticated drinker, the nose is the sorter of sensations. It distributes the appetite to the nerve cells that will later flourish upon the crevices of the tongue and palate in sensory abundance.

With these principles established, the most perfect glass is undoubtedly that whose crystal belly closely resembles a sphere. Exquisitely delicate wine glasses do exist. Often, and this is ideal, the transparent belly narrows at the top to direct the wine's bouquet towards the nostrils. These kinds of glasses also create a larger surface for evaporation, and nothing gets lost from these aromas that render life more beautiful for the subtle nose!

In my opinion, the hierarchy of glasses and their economical usage is blasphemy. At a dinner party, you generally sit down at table before a complete medley of glasses, the largest of which is the water glass. Why does water get to enjoy this privilege? Alfred Jarry said that water is such an impure liquid that only one drop is needed to ruin an entire glass of absinthe! I don't go that far; I don't have anything against water. It's a respectable liquid. Still, it's not wine. Consequently, how, upon a serious table, can the receptacle attracting the most attention be dedicated for water? Should guests taste the "Château Water Tower?" This tradition is irrational and we should do away with such an inelegant habit. A water glass? If need be! Sometimes

a passive mouthful of water makes certain luxuries worth it. But water glasses shouldn't take up more space than others. They don't merit any particular consideration.

Furthermore, I have never been able to understand how, at fancy dinners, a glass for Bordeaux is smaller than a water glass, and larger than a Bourgogne glass. Why? Purely tradition, or to be more precise, irrational tradition!

Why?

It doesn't correspond to any logic, nor does it correspond to simple convenience.

Whatever they may be, our greatest wines are gifted with diverse aromas and beautiful nuances. To serve these pleasures while diminishing them with a too-small glass is a cruel joke. All the senses should be engaged and delighted by a noble wine, a feedback loop of the joys of the gaze, nose, tongue, palate, and the mind—disrupting the nasal yield with a too-small glass destroys one of the essential elements of a wine's lushness.

With the preceding laws established, there is yet another: never fill more than half the glass. Stay below, well below, because the little genie in the bottle will enjoy all his delights and freely frolic for your nose's satisfaction, and life's graces.

To summarize, a good stemmed glass should be of a comfortable size, fine, light, balanced, well placed at table, and without engravings, or facets. The bowl, or globe, shouldn't flare out, but, on the contrary, it should narrow into a tulip-like shape. Neither squared, nor hexagonal, nor octagonal, it soberly remains cylindrical. The height of the stem, leg and base included, should be slightly smaller than that of the bowl by two-thirds or three-fourths, and never greater. The base should only ever be round.

Such is the "canon" of a tasteful glass.

I've noticed certain gourmands have taken up the habit of serving fine wines in even more styles of glasses; I shall present one example. When it's of high quality, fine champagne flourishes in huge coupes, but for wine, we can critique their usage. Whites oxidize too fast and lose their freshness too quickly; slightly delicate reds don't sufficiently concentrate their delicacy before the nasal test.

And now, a general rule: when an artist designs a glass, he should remind himself that it's not Monseigneur le Vin who should adapt himself to the glass, but that it's the glass that should give in to Monseigneur le Vin's demands!

Monseigneur le Vin

Adaptations

Hosts are often embarrassed when they have to serve several wines alongside several dishes.

Which one to serve first?

Nobody can deny that a beautiful Saint-Émilion or, even better, a great Bourgogne showcases a wonderful Roquefort. Reciprocity is real.

We can resolve a problem that gourmets have disputed for eternity, just as baccarat players debate argue the finer points of the game:

"Should you serve the dessert before cheese, or should the cheese go first?"

In theory, and in general, the order is: *savory, sweet.* The savory dish precedes the sweet one.

If this rule reigns supreme, cheese must be served before dessert. This is the opinion of M. Charles Maurice de Talleyrand, a great cheese gourmand, the only diet to which he adhered all his life.

But in practice, one can be of another opinion . . . The response depends on the guests . . . If they're wine lovers, don't hesitate: serve the cheese at the end, because for the wine connoisseur, the aroma of a great red wine merging with that of a mature mix of fermented milk is the very key to paradise . . . In this case, dessert *is* the wine.

But if your guests aren't high-level insiders, simply take the red wines away, serve the dessert after the cheese, and accompany it with a delicate white wine or a sweet fortified wine . . .

Another issue: Should the wines be varied during a large meal? Paul says: *oui*. Pierre says: *non*. I think it's better to say: *oui*. Except for champagne, wine's effects dull rather quickly; variety and choice thus become necessary. But I must add that certain wines, when the food suits them, perfectly stay the course from the beginning to the end of the meal.

———

Several General Rules

A. — Avoid complex wines before lighter or less full-bodied wines, for example, a red Bourgogne before a red Bordeaux, a Porto before a Bourgogne or a Bordeaux.

B. — Avoid sweeter wines before dry ones, for example, a Sauternes or an Anjou before a Chablis.

C. — Avoid red wine after a fortified white wine, for example, a red Bordeaux after a Sauternes, a Château-Margaux after a Château-Yquem.

Faites enlever les verres

D. — Throw out any guests who mix their wines.

LE VIN LE PLUS FORT CHASSE LE PLUS dELICAT

Never see these people again. If for any reason you need to spare these barbarians, gradually remove their glasses during the service, even if they're still full. It's a pity that so-called "manners" forbid this kind of behavior. When the gourmands rule, this custom will become a form of politeness.

These directives don't require explanation. The strongest wine chases the most delicate; white wines from Sauternes and Anjou have the most sugar, and therefore more sweetness than red wines, so the latter seem diminished when they follow the former, etc.

In sum, it's simple.

* The strongest wine chases the more delicate wine

And yet, how many consumers, how many industry men even, ignore this elementary rule, and are barbaric enough to recommend serving Madeira, Xérès, or Porto before a meal or with . . . soup!

Let's weep! Imposing the palate with a choice of this sort at the beginning of a dinner results in a brutalization of the remaining dishes. The taste buds will make a huge effort to "recover," as athletes say, following this punch to the gut.

Down with indulgence that's a hypocritical manifestation of spinelessness, of weakness, in the presence of bad habits! Learn to follow these wise and simple rules.

Just think about it, and your good senses will be thankful for these several considerations!

The Development of Flavors

Wine and food should mutually highlight each another. It would be idiotic to have a battle of flavors while all the happiness on Earth can be achieved within their harmonic balance. Therefore, red Bordeaux wines clash with dishes with too much vinegar, or too much sugar . . . The easiest of experiments demonstrates this.

But how an aged red wine enhances crawfish! A lyrical prose writer, Maurice des Ombiaux, guarantees that if pastries and fruit don't pair well with red Bourgognes, that in summertime the sensation is magnificent when a rare wine of the Côte-d'Or accompanies a fresh slice of melon!

Several examples will clarify these issues, vast like the world, varied like humanity, so sweet to experience!

Fish calls for white wine, except when it's served with matelote, a delectable fish stew prepared with red wine. Chablis and Pouilly seem to have been created to accompany oysters and chilled seafood.

A Haut-Barsac, or a dry, white Bourgogne perfectly harmonize with warm fish.

A Montrachet deifies galantine, ham, and cold poultry . . .

Certain individuals, but I don't really share this viewpoint, believe that Porto can accompany lobster à l'Armoricaine (or, as others call it, *à l'américaine*) with crawfish, timbales, and plenty of pepper and spices.

If it's good quality, a fortified Madeira wine pairs with fruit or dessert.

According to the rules, you shouldn't keep serving red wine until dessert, except for the aforementioned exception with regards to the cheese tasters who are fatal friends of Bourgogne and Saint-Émilion, unless they have a weakness for l'Hermitage or a Châteauneuf-du-Pape.

As already explained, dessert reaches its pinnacle with sweet white wines from Bordeaux, and certain Anjous, several of which are so pleasant, and with certain wines from Touraine, several of which are so rare.

Warmed or slightly fermented cheeses are friends with Meursault, Alsatian wine, and white wine from Moselle.

And what more do I know?

As for champagne, if it's dry, it accompanies an entire meal, but you shouldn't offer it after cheese or dessert . . . However, at fancy banquets where a coupe—ah! I lament the old flute that lets stars appear within wine—where a coupe, I was saying, aids with toasts, speeches, and talks, champagne is the final touch. In these conditions, it's best light and subtly sweet, with fruit and candies.

To summarize, the custom of serving champagne at the end of a meal might seem heretical. This type of wine, let's shout it from the rooftops, should precede all other wines, and it's at the beginning of a meal that it should be offered, semi-dry or dry, of course. If you keep it out throughout an entire dinner, you can vary and harmonize its effects, by transitioning from a dry champagne to a semi-dry, to finish with the sweetest, just before dessert.

Let's hasten to proclaim: the laws that I have just explained aren't narrow, unforgiving legislation. You must follow your spirit rather than the law. Hosts who respect their guests enough to analyze their selected dishes and present them in a smart order has the right, being familiar with the wines in their cellars, to vary the pleasures according to affinities only they know . . . The wine service should be a symphony!

Le service des vins doit être une symphonie

* Wine service must be a symphony

A controversial question remains:

What should be served with various hors-d'oeuvres, oil-based condiments, Turkish-style eggplant, artichoke hearts, diced mixed vegetables in mayonnaise, etc.?

In the presence of hors-d'oeuvres whose taste is acidic or bold, the best wine abandons the battlefield.

It reveals itself as annihilated, flattened . . . Even worse! All its charm seems deformed . . . Pardon me for this harsh comparison, but it's like a beautiful fedora, destroyed by a punch!

Several portents are whispered in your ear: "With these kinds of hors-d'oeuvres serve a small, aggressive gray wine, harvested in the Aube or Lorraine!"

Maybe, if you wish. But perhaps there's a better way.

Two solutions present themselves. I'll whisper them in your ear, very quietly. I'd have too many enemies if I revealed them out loud.

Here's the first:

To avoid embarrassment, when you're asking yourself which type of wine to serve in this case, there's a good solution: don't serve any hors-d'oeuvres!

As far as I'm concerned, I don't really like them. Most often, they owe their essential flavor to vinegar, which is just sour wine. It's precisely because it's sour wine that vinegar accepts being paired with wine that *didn't* go bad with little indulgence. In a family, he who hasn't succeeded holds it against his happy parents; this is the case for vinegar, the sickly enemy of his healthy brother.

Here's the second solution:

If you absolutely must have hors-d'oeuvres and if you're looking for a beverage that conforms to their gustatory esthetic, instead of wine, pour . . . water. Yes, good, fresh water, clear, light . . .

Il a mal tourné

To complement the hors-d'oeuvres, water is best, water that washes the palate, thus disposing it to the most classic sensations that result.

So that you fully understand me:

My disdain of hors-d'oeuvres isn't about scorning certain various distractions, which can be usually warm, simple pastries to which the great culinary artists assign unexpected, attractive, spiritual shapes.

No, I only protest against acidic or gelatinous hors-d'oeuvres that take part in the art of accommodating leftovers far too often . . .

* A bad seed

Water!

In the same vein of thought, which wine can accompany salad? I can't think of any. Thus, it's better not to drink during this formality, which is in service to certain hygienic habits, but which numerous gourmets banish from their tables because it can needlessly harm the wine service.

* Water!

Dishes to recommend and to banish

With red wine

Recommended dishes:

Ham croustades with cheese.
Kidney skewers with bacon.
Lamb.
Mutton.
Beef.
Veal.
Poultry.
Game.
Starchy vegetables.
Cep mushrooms.
Game pâtés.
Foie gras pâtés.
Cheshire, gruyere, Roquefort, semi-hard Dutch cheese,
half-salted Emmental, and Camembert.

Dishes to banish:

Hors-d'oeuvres with vinegar.
Crustaceans.
Eggs.
Pasta (noodles, macaroni).
White sauces and Madeira sauces.
Green vegetables except for ceps.
Salads and dishes with vinegar.
Creamy cheeses.
Sweet dishes, whatever they may be.

Certain dishes call for light, aromatic wines, and others for bold
wines with a very pronounced taste.

Dishes to recommend and to banish

With white wine

Recommended dishes:

Oysters.
Cold and warm fish.
Armorican langoustine.
Timbales and savory puff pastries.
Sweetbreads.
Roasted poultry.
Chicken and rice.
Lamb.
Ham.
Foie gras aspic.
Galantine.
Desserts and iced cakes.
Light cheeses.
Roasted almonds.

Dishes to banish:

Hors-d'oeuvres with vinegar.
Roast beef.
Madeira sauce.
Vegetables with cream.
Salads and dishes with vinegar.
Heavy, creamy cheeses.

With oysters and fish, flavorful dry or semi-dry wines are preferred; with meat, fortified wines, and with dessert, very fortified wines.

USAGE ACCORDING TO DIFFERENT DISHES

———

1. Red Wine :
a) Light.
b) Full-bodied.

2. White Wine :
a) Dry.
b) Sweet or semi-dry.

1. RED WINES

a) Dishes with which LIGHT wines are preferred:

Ham croustades with cheese.
Kidney skewers with bacon.
Lamb chops.
Leg of mutton.
Saddle of lamb.
Lamb Villeroy.
Roasted veal.
Sweetbreads.
Grilled mutton chops.

Poultry giblets.
Roast skylark.
Roast quail.
Roast turkey poult.
Roast thrush.

Roast partridge.
Roast pigeon.
Roast guinea fowl.
Roast chicken.
Chicken in a pot.

Flageolet beans.
Braised lettuce.
Lentils.
Peas.
"Maître d'hôtel" potatoes
Potatoes with butter.

Foie gras.
Pâtés of the above meats.

b) Dishes with which FULL-BODIED or vigorous wines are necessary:

Leg of lamb with green beans.
Mutton ragout.
Saddle of mutton with mixed
   vegetables.

Beef — beefsteak, Périgueux filet mignon, filet and sirloin, rump steak, grilled rounds of beef, Rossini rounds of beef.

Duck — roasted, Rouen-style, with olives, with turnips.

Goose cassoulet.
Périgueux duck livers.
Butterflied pigeon.

Chicken — hunter's chicken, Marengo.

Woodcock.
Snipe.
Venison.
Pheasant.
Hare.
Partridge with cabbage.
Wild boar.
Duck.

Artichoke thistle au jus.
Braised or au jus celery.
Bordeaux ceps.
Cauliflower au gratin.
Artichoke hearts.
String beans with lardons.
Potatoes with lardons.

Pâtés of the above meats.

2. WHITE WINES

a) Dishes with which DRY white wines are preferred:

Oysters, shellfish.

Eggs.

Lobster or langoustine with mayonnaise.

Cold fish with mayonnaise.

– grilled.

– fried.

Roasted poultry.

Duck with olives.

– with turnips.

Roast lamb.

Braised lettuce.

Braised celery.

Braised endives.

Braised turnips.

Cauliflower au gratin.

Crawfish.

Galantine.

Ham.

Iced cakes.

b) Dishes with which SWEET or semi-dry wines are preferred:

Puff pastries.

Sweetbreads.

Timbales.

Caen-style tripe.

Vol-au-vents.

Bouillabaisse.

Lobster Armorican.

Normandy sole.

Fish with white sauce.

– heavy or semi-heavy.

Sautéed chicken.

– Marengo.

– Hunter's

Chicken with rice.

Asparagus with white sauce.

Artichoke thistle.

Flageolet beans.

Artichoke hearts.

Green beans.

Lentils.

Noodles and macaroni.

Peas.

Potatoes.

Foie gras.

Desserts.

The Wine Service

	Service No. 1 with only red BORDEAUX	Service No. 2 with only red BOURGOGNE	Service No. 3 with only white BORDEAUX	Service No. 4 with only white BOURGOGNE
Appropriate APPETIZER	Light MÉDOC or GRAVES	BEAUJOLAIS	Dry haut BARSAC	CHABLIS or POUILLY
Appropriate ROASTS and VEGETABLES	Very rich grand MÉDOC or GRAVES	Light grand BOURGOGNE		MEURSAULT
Appropriate COLD DISH		Full-bodied grand BOURGOGNE	sweet SAUTERNES	MONTRACHET
Appropriate CHEESE	very full-bodied St.-ÉMILION or POMEROL			
DESSERT	Forbidden	No!	Very fortified grand SAUTERNES	Don't even think about it

80

The Wine Service

	Service No. 5 with only CHAMPAGNE	Service No. 6 with TOURAINE and ANJOU	Service No. 7 with only white ANJOU	Service No. 8 with red BORDEAUX and white BORDEAUX
Appropriate APPETIZER	dry CHAMPAGNE	CHINON	CHÂTEAU DU BREUIL	MÉDOC, GRAVES, or St.-ÉMILION
Appropriate ROASTS		St.-NICOLAS de BOURGUEIL		
Appropriate COLD DISH		CHAMPIGNY (red wine from the Saumurois)	CHÂTEAU D'ÉPIRÉ	
Appropriate CHEESE	Sweet CHAMPAGNE			
DESSERT		VOUVRAY	QUART DE CHAUME	SAUTERNES or BARSAC

The Wine Service

	Service No. 9 with white BOURGOGNE and red BOURGOGNE	Service No. 10 CHAMPAGNE and BORDEAUX	Service No. 11 varied	Service No. 12 varied
Appropriate APPETIZER	CHABLIS, POUILLY, MEURSAULT, or MONTRACHET	dry CHAMPAGNE	dry CHAMPAGNE, MOSELLE, CHABLIS, POUILLY, or MEURSAULT	red TOURAINE or light red BORDEAUX
Appropriate ROAST	light red BOURGOGNE	light BORDEAUX	Grand red BORDEAUX or grand red BOURGOGNE	Grand red BOURGOGNE or CÔTES du RHÔNE
Appropriate COLD DISH		very rich BORDEAUX		
Appropriate CHEESE	Grand, full-bodied red BOURGOGNE	very rich St.–ÉMILION		
DESSERT	Nope	Grand SAUTERNES	Grand MADEIRA or PORTO	sweet grand ANJOU

The Wine Service

	Service No. 13 varied	Service No. 14 varied	Service No. 15 varied	Service No. 16 varied
Appropriate APPETIZER	semi-dry CHAMPAGNE or JURANÇON or a semi-dry and light BARSAC	dry CHAMPAGNE or MOSELLE (Traminer)	POUILLY	dry CHAMPAGNE
Appropriate ROAST	Very rich St.-ÉMILION	red BEAUJOLAIS		semi-dry white BORDEAUX
Appropriate COLD DISH		red BOURGOGNE	Grand MONTRACHET	Grand red BOURGOGNE
Appropriate CHEESE				Grand red BORDEAUX
DESSERT	Grand MALVOISIE	sweet grand ANJOUE	dry and iced aged JEREZ	Grand SAUTERNES

PART THREE

Drink

CHAPTER V

Drinking Wine

The attitude

This is an important chapter, worthy of meditation.

It will reveal the essential difference between a simple ingurgitation and the art of drinking.

Connoisseurs distinguishes themselves via attitude . . . They possess a special upholding. M. Mathieu, the famous professor of oenology, described it in perfect terms. Here, I shall borrow several words from him (because one borrows only from the rich), and I'll summarize.

Mental Preparation

Drinkers dedicate themselves to drinking. They concentrate all of their attentive faculties upon their drink.

Préparation mentale

* Mental preparation

Pleasure of the Eyes

The glass is half full. The Drinker leans over in such a way to rejoice in the colors, by varying the layers of liquid. He admires the nuances that go from white, golden, pink, to ruby red, to onion peel, or even yellow straw, where certain plays of light sometimes add a ray of emerald.

Plaisir des yeux

* Pleasure of the eyes

Pleasure of the Nose
and Brain

A. — With the surface of wine being horizontal, one gently inhales to "smell the bouquets." *B.* — By progressively rotating the liquid, the olfactory effect intensifies. This dance favors the manifestation of evaporative principles through agitation and contact with air.

For this gyratory movement, the law and its adherents recommend delicately taking the glass's bowl between the thumb and index finger, with the three other fingers free and slightly fanned out, and to then rotate it in a counterclockwise direction. This agitation transforms the wine's surface from horizontal to parabolic, and coats the free part of the glass with wine. Thus, the olfactory qualities expand via the variety of scents, some of them subtle, some of them strong. Furthermore, the connoisseur endeavors to recognize and characterize them, to compare them to previously detected bouquets. It's a delectable moment.

Plaisir du nez

Pleasures of the Mouth, Tongue, and Palate

Next, you drink delicately, in small sips, just as birds do. Each mouthful is taken in order to better analyze it; each area of the tongue has specialized sensitivities. You must know that the "beaches of the tongue each have specialized sensitivities." The cultivated taster doesn't miss out on this moment to make a "mixing bowl" of his mouth. They inhale a bit of air to mingle with the wine in the mouth. At this moment, a new series of scents and flavors rise from the glass to the superior regions of the intellect.

Plaisir de la bouche

* Pleasure of the mouth

Now the majestic, religious, ideal, definitive moment begins, that of

The Appreciation

The head tilts, the face becomes serious, and, in the depths of their soul, collecting their memories, gathering via intelligence, remembered sensations, the drinker assumes the role of judge. Then, one discusses, one compares.

A prodigal expert, the tongue, the human organ possessing the most memory, remembers tastings from thirty, forty years ago. Through time, it sorts through tastes that were long thought forgotten; it classifies them, in the delicate manner of tapestry artists who discover the brotherly thread in the correct color through one thousand tangles.

L'appréciation

This quick classification of old sensations and memories is, for wine, the greatest part of the art form. It's what distinguishes the connoisseur and the champion.

And, of course, aficionados compare the ages of the bottles. They know the good years. Without reverting back to the famous year of the Comète (1811), they cite and respectfully evoke:

1858–1864–1869–1875– 1878–1899–1900–1916	for red Bordeaux.
1861–1869–1871–1874–1893– 1900–1901–1904–1908	for white Bordeaux.
1865–1870–1881–1904– 1906–1911–1915	for Bourgognes.
1889–1893–1904–1906– 1911–1915	for Champagne.

Then the connoisseurs share their opinions, which remain mysterious for the laymen. The ignorant or badly civilized person doesn't understand that a wine with "the hat on the ear," meaning a wine that's too old, is a liquid in which a sharpness pierces—the beginning of a downfall. A wine with the "waistcoat" is an opulent wine, well constituted, male, the wine of a serious man in good health, whereas the wine with the "bodice" is more delicate, feminine, well done, finer, more in love . . .

In general, the gourmands of the highest order satisfy themselves by distinguishing "the body," "the color," "the softness," or the "dryness," "the lifeblood," "the bouquet," and "the odor." The connoisseurs of a higher degree are

1811

naturally armed with a richer language, and their imagination dictates new vocabulary with each drop . . .

Just as with "color," there are one hundred expressions that are more striking or beautiful than the previous. They describe the various nature-like nuances, and measure innumerable

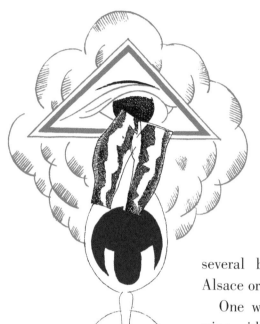

transparent details . . . The range runs from white to yellow, to red, to brown, to clear amber to oxblood to ruby, then transitioning to aged gold to rose without being red, golden without being yellow, which charms in several bottles coming from Alsace or the Côtes du Rhône.

One would say that a rich wine with a bouquet "extends itself" or even "struts its stuff in the mouth." "A delicious expression," writes a very distinguished member of the Agriculture Academy, M. Prosper Gervais, who, in his charming way, admirably translates what one experiences: "By receiving this lifeblood, the sensation of an infinite delicacy first provokes a sense of amazement and slowly deploys itself, develops, and amplifies until it bathes the palate's sails and the entire mouth with its subtle aroma."

For sure, old people don't miss out when wine flows, remembering one of those numerous proverbs that, according to the locale, extol wine's benefits, its blessings, its graces.

Thus, when a sweet Sauternes wine is consumed, one shouldn't begin drinking it without first invoking that old adage "it's the good Lord that descends from the heavens in velvet underpants."

This charming expression is also used in Bourgogne.

Social joy — These magic movements, these shared words, these comparisons, these judgments, these memories, inspire contentment in life.

At this moment, man can proclaim: "I am happy."

It's happiness through enthusiasm that, from ἐν Θεός, means: God is within me.

The Vocabulary

To describe a wine, there is room to consider:

1. *The general constitution:* the body, the fineness, the equilibrium;

2. *The vinosity;*

3. *The color, the hue;*

4. *The sweetness or the hardness* resulting from the content of sugar, acid, scale, tannins, etc.;

5. *The bouquet and the flavor:* the bouquet resulting from the essential ethers perceived by the sense of smell, the flavor resulting from the essential ethers perceived through taste.

1. THE GENERAL CONSTITUTION, THE BODY, THE FINENESS

Vocabulary of qualities

A complete, enriched wine.
— Full-bodied.
— Fleshy, well-fleshed.
— Muscled.
— Husky, fleshed out.
— Full, nourished.
— Well seated.
— Robust, vigorous.
— Well-balanced.
— Has body.
— Has meat.
— Has consistency.
— Has base.
— Has depth.
— Has structure.
— Has support.
What a giant!
A wine that has stomach.
— Has a waistcoat.
— Has a blouse.

Vocabulary of faults

Thin wine.
— Weakling.

— Skimpy.
— Thin, a breadboard.

— Badly balanced.
— Off color, badly
constructed.
— Lanky.

QUIA DU CORSAGE

104   *Has a blouse*

Fine, delicate wine.

— Loving, elegant.
— Serious, having manners.
— Has character.
— Has color.
A great Lord!

Impolite wine.
— Common.
— Frivolous, with bells and whistles.

A Plebian.
Boorish.

2. THE VINOSITY

Vigorous wine.
— Intoxicating.
— Strong.

— Generous.
— Has heat.
— Has fire.
— Close-grained.

Soft wine.
— Flat.
— Limp.
— Weak, lymphatic.
— Poor.

Cold wine.
— Anemic, sickly.

QUI EST FLASQUE

*Is flabby

3. THE COLOR, THE HUE

Brilliant wine.   Sordid wine.

— Scintillating.   — Broken.
— Full of color.   — Drab.
— Amber.   — Weighted down.
— Ruby.
— Golden-brown.   — Having too much color.
— Tawny.
— Nude.   — Overdressed.
— Onion peel.
— Has a pretty color.   — Having an ugly color.
— Looks sharp.   — Badly dressed.

4. THE SOFTNESS, THE HARDNESS

A clear wine.

— Has bouquet.
— Has nose.
— Scented.
— Notes of truffle,
raspberry, etc.
— Taste of nuts, peach, etc.
— Thick texture,
has lifeblood.
— Very syrupy.

— Well-conserved, stays
the course.

— Fruity.
— Flavorful.
— Alive.
— Sharp.
— Brazen.
— Perky.
— Alluring, bawdy.
— Debauched, ahoy!
— Ahoy!
— Prolongs itself.
— Attractive.

A sickly, weak wine.

— Flat.

— Rancid.
— With the taste of a
  fox's tail.
— Tired, used.
— Old.
— Plunging.
— Past.

— Thin, scrawny.
— Dead.
— Wilted.
— Extinguished.

— Flattened.
— Doughy.
— Heavy.
— Thick, chewed.
— Drab.
— Bothersome.

— Finishes short.
— Dumb.

QUI A LE CHAPEAU
SUR L'OREILLE.

Wears a hat over the ears

Exciting wine.

— Seductive.
— Evocative.
— A go-getter.
— In love.
— Sensual.
— Voluptuous.
— Hot.
— Full of panache.
— Struts its stuff.
— Speaks well.
— Sings.
— Affluent, with a chic finish.

Insignificant wine.

— Without charm.
— Without attraction.

— Severe.
— Austere, sour.

— Mute.
— Disheveled, frilly.

QUİ A du CHİEN

CONCLUSION

Be Careful About Whom You Offer It To

And now, a fundamental recommendation. It's sacrilegious to offer a great wine to just anybody.

It's throwing pearls to swine. One offers the most esteemed bottles only to connoisseurs who are able to appreciate them, and, if necessary, to young individuals gifted with the sort of interior sophistication that allows them to strive for a complete education in the realm of taste one day.

Pierre de Ronsard, one of our most gracious poets, was born in Couture, in Touraine. His father, the knighted Loys de Ronsard, had a charming manor house there, the abode of a spiritual scholar. He was a boisterous and gay master, but measured, as befits a polite gentleman who knows that things are enjoyed best in moderation, and that one must not ignore the pious precepts that advise avoiding excess. Thus, his home was brimming with dignity and taste. Each object had its place, with the kind of disposition of the learned, when they have a talent for decorating, who know how to ennoble their home.

For example, you could admire a beautiful chapel for the church of the Lord, a beautiful kitchen for the church of the body, and a double wine cellar for the simultaneous church of both.

As in the rest of the house, the wine cellar was embellished with inscriptions in stone. They remain today; you can still decipher and decode these lapidary philosophical mottos. One can read, for example: "Before departing."

These two words mean that the lord of the manor wished to taste as much as possible the fruits of the land before his moment of passing. This maxim, "Before departing," was found sculpted at the entrance of the fine wine vault. This reminds me of one of my friends who, looking to reconnect with his soul, took out an old, fine bottle of Bourgogne that he kept for a special occasion, and said: "I won't leave this in my will . . . Look how a man who'll go digest in another world drinks!"

He, too, wanted to taste his fine wine "Before departing"!

Loys de Ronsard's wine cellar was divided in two. The maxim *Vinum Barbarum* was found on one side of the cellar. This shouldn't be translated as Barbaric wine. The phrase simply means Ordinary wine.

AVANT
PARTIR

The rare wine vault was just next door. It was decorated with an inscription that I ask you to meditate on, because it's the one that makes these final lines marrying history and wine poetry worth it for you. It read: *Cui des Videto.*

"Be careful about whom you offer it to."

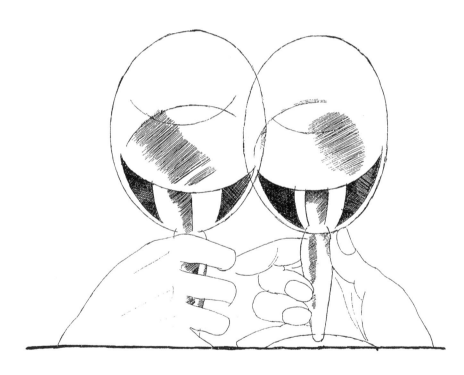

And now that I, dear reader, have taught you, to the best of my abilities, how to drink according to the grand traditions, let us clink our glasses and toast in the time-honored way:

> Me: To your health!
> You: And to yours.
> Me: Wholeheartedly!
> You: Indeed.

And both together: Cheers!

ORIGINALLY PRINTED ON THE PRESSES

OF

THE DRAEGER BROTHERS

FOR THE NICOLAS ESTABLISHMENTS

PARIS

NOVEMBER 1927

Published in the United States of America in 2020 by
RIZZOLI INTERNATIONAL PUBLICATIONS, INC.
300 Park Avenue South
New York, NY 10010
www.rizzoliusa.com

First published in 1927 by Établissements Nicolas

Publisher: Charles Miers
Editor: Jessica Fuller
Translation: Victorine Lamothe
Design: Kayleigh Jankowski
Copyeditor: Victoria Brown
Managing Editor: Lynn Scrabis
Production Manager: Kaija Markoe

SPECIAL THANKS TO
Carmella Abramowitz Moreau, Christophe Hermelin, and Nicolas

PRINTED IN HONG KONG

2020 2021 2022 2023 / 10 9 8 7 6 5 4 3 2 1

ISBN: 978-0-7893-3800-6
Library of Congress Control Number: 2019917113

VISIT US ONLINE:
Facebook.com/RizzoliNewYork
Twitter: @Rizzoli_Books
Instagram.com/RizzoliBooks
Pinterest.com/RizzoliBooks
Youtube.com/user/RizzoliNY
Issuu.com/Rizzoli

About the original book

Monseigneur Le Vin: L'art de boire was originally one of a set of five promotional volumes published 1924–1927 by French wine distributor Maison Nicolas. Published in French in 1927, *Monseigneur Le Vin* was written by Louis Forest (1872–1933), a celebrated journalist, playwright, and novelist, and was designed and illustrated by Charles Martin (1834–1934), best known for his work in *Gazette du Bon Ton*, *Modes et Manières d'Aujourd'hui*, *Journal Des Dames et Des Modes*, and *Vogue*.